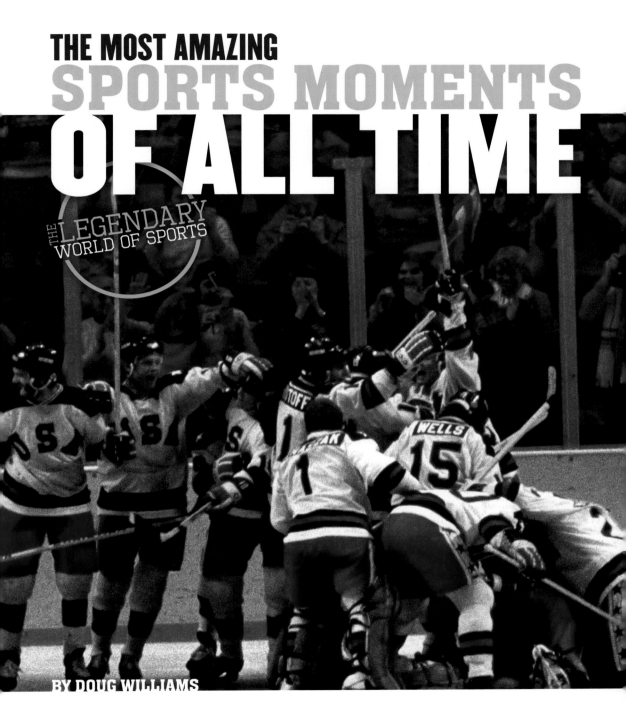

THE MOST AMAZING
SPORTS MOMENTS
OF ALL TIME

THE LEGENDARY WORLD OF SPORTS

BY DOUG WILLIAMS

SportsZone
An Imprint of Abdo Publishing | abdopublishing.com

abdopublishing.com

Published by Abdo Publishing, a division of ABDO, PO Box 398166, Minneapolis, Minnesota 55439. Copyright © 2016 by Abdo Consulting Group, Inc. International copyrights reserved in all countries. No part of this book may be reproduced in any form without written permission from the publisher. SportsZone™ is a trademark and logo of Abdo Publishing.

Printed in the United States of America, North Mankato, Minnesota
082015
012016

 THIS BOOK CONTAINS RECYCLED MATERIALS

Cover Photo: AP Images
Interior Photos: AP Images, 1, 6, 10; John Rooney/AP Images, 4; Harry Harris/AP Images, 8; A. E. Maloof/AP Images, 13; IHA/Icon SMI 524/IHA/Icon SMI/Newscom, 15; Arthur Anderson/AP Images, 16; G. Newman Lowrance/AP Images, 18; Carl Viti/AP Images, 20, 22; Carol Francavilla/AP Images, 24; Amy Sancetta/AP Images, 26, 28; John Gaps III/AP Images, 30; Mark J. Terrill/AP Images, 33; Petr David Josek/AP Images, 35; Jeff Roberson/AP Images, 36; Matt Slocum/AP Images, 38; Lynne Sladky/AP Images, 40, 43; Dave Martin/AP Images, 45

Editor: Patrick Donnelly
Series Designer: Nikki Farinella

Library of Congress Control Number: 2015945545

Cataloging-in-Publication Data
Williams, Doug.
 The most amazing sports moments of all time / Doug Williams.
   p. cm. -- (The legendary world of sports)
 ISBN 978-1-62403-990-4 (lib. bdg.)
 Includes bibliographical references and index.
 1. Sports--Records--Juvenile literature. 2. Sports--Miscellanea--Juvenile
literature. I. Title.
 796--dc23
                                                          2015945545

TABLE OF CONTENTS

1947
ROBINSON'S DEBUT

On the afternoon of April 15, 1947, Jackie Robinson made history. He did not hit a game-winning home run. He did not break a record. He merely put on his first baseman's mitt and jogged to his position in the top of the first inning.

With that simple act, baseball's color barrier had been broken.

For more than 60 years, no black player had played a Major League Baseball (MLB) game. Team owners had followed an unwritten rule that the big leagues would be for whites only. But the Brooklyn Dodgers decided to break that rule. Dodgers executive Branch Rickey signed Robinson, a three-sport star at the

Jackie Robinson poses in his Brooklyn Dodgers uniform.

Jackie Robinson shows his form at first base.

University of California, Los Angeles (UCLA). Rickey liked Robinson's talent. He liked his maturity too. He thought Robinson would be able stay calm and focused while facing the ugly racism he was sure to encounter.

On Opening Day of the 1947 season at Ebbets Field in Brooklyn, Robinson played first base and hit second in the Dodgers lineup. He did not get a hit, but he scored the winning run in a 5–3 victory over the Boston Braves.

More importantly, Robinson showed he belonged. He went on to play 10 seasons in a Hall of Fame career. In 1947 he hit .297, stole a league-best 29 bases, and was voted Rookie of the Year. He endured racist taunts from fans and even other players, yet he held his temper. By playing with dignity and grace, Robinson opened doors for other black players.

"It was just another ballgame, and that's the way they're all going to be," he said after his debut in Brooklyn. But it was much more than that. The moment Robinson stepped on the field, baseball was changed forever.

2

1960
MAZ BLASTS WALK-OFF

Bill Mazeroski was known for his defense. The Pittsburgh Pirates' second baseman won eight Gold Gloves for fielding excellence. But on the afternoon of October 13, 1960, Mazeroski became a legend with his bat.

The Pirates and New York Yankees were dueling in Game 7 of the World Series. The Yankees scored two runs in the top of the ninth inning to tie the game 9–9.

The Yankees had the star power with Hall of Fame sluggers such as Mickey Mantle and Yogi Berra in the lineup. Going into the bottom of the ninth, they had outscored the Pirates 55–26 in the seven games. Their

Bill Mazeroski, *center*, is mobbed after his game-winning home run in Game 7 of the 1960 World Series.

Don Larsen delivers a pitch during his perfect game in the 1956 World Series.

three victories were by scores of 16–3, 10–0, and 12–0. The Pirates had won three games by a total of six runs.

Game 7 was another close one. Advantage: Pirates. Mazeroski led off the ninth for Pittsburgh. On the second pitch from New York's Ralph Terry, he swung.

The ball soared. It disappeared over the 406-foot sign in left-center field.

As Mazeroski rounded the bases, he waved his arms in excitement. By the time he touched third base, fans were streaming onto the field. At home plate he was mobbed by teammates and fans. It was the first—and through 2014, still the only—time a World Series Game 7 had ended on a walk-off home run.

"From second to home, I never touched the ground," said Mazeroski. "I just floated around there."

WORLD SERIES PERFECTION

Four years before Mazeroski's feat, Don Larsen did something no other pitcher has ever done in a World Series. On October 8, 1956, the Yankees' Larsen threw a perfect game. He retired all 27 batters he faced in a 2–0 win over Brooklyn. "When it was over, I was so happy I felt like crying," said Larsen.

1970
ORR GOES AIRBORNE

The moment is frozen in time. Bobby Orr is horizontal, three feet above the ice. He is screaming in celebration. His stick is raised in triumph. Behind him, Bruins fans are pumping their arms and cheering. They know their team has just won the Stanley Cup.

It is one of the most famous photos in American sports. It was snapped at the instant Orr turned into Superman.

On the afternoon of May 10, 1970, Orr and the Bruins were playing the St. Louis Blues. It was Game 4 of the Stanley Cup Finals. The Bruins had won the first three games. Now Boston was just a win away from its first National Hockey League (NHL) championship

Bobby Orr, *left*, takes a dive after scoring the goal that clinched the 1970 Stanley Cup.

since 1941. The Blues, however, would not quit. The game went to overtime tied 3–3. Then Orr soared.

Seconds into overtime, Orr controlled a loose puck and charged up the ice. He passed to teammate Derek Sanderson in the corner. Orr then skated toward the Blues' net. The return pass to Orr was perfect. He slapped the puck past goalie Glenn Hall.

Orr was tripped just after he shot. He went airborne. The photograph of a flying Orr was a big hit coast to coast. In 2010 the image became a bronze statue outside the Bruins' arena. And both Orr and the photo have a spot in the Hockey Hall of Fame.

1980
ERUZIONE'S GOLDEN GOAL

In 1980 the Soviet Union's hockey team was the most powerful on Earth. It was made up of veteran stars. The Soviets had won every Olympics since 1964. They had not lost an Olympic game since 1968.

In 1979 the Soviets beat a team of NHL all-stars 6–0. Just before the 1980 Olympics began at Lake Placid, New York, the Soviets routed Team USA 10–3. So when the Americans met the Soviets in the medal round of the Olympics, the US team was a huge underdog.

Yet the Americans—mostly college players—would not roll over. Going into the third period, the Soviets led 3–2. Mark Johnson's second goal of the game made it 3–3. With 10 minutes left, US captain Mike Eruzione gave his team the lead. Eruzione, 25, was an

US players celebrate during their victory over Finland that clinched the 1980 Olympic hockey gold medal.

unlikely hero. He was a former minor league player from Boston University. He would never play in the NHL. But on that day in Lake Placid, he made history.

His shot from 25 feet away beat Soviet goaltender Vladimir Myshkin. Now leading 4–3, Team USA held off waves of Soviet attacks. US goaltender Jim Craig stopped shot after shot. When the game ended, the Americans swarmed onto the ice in triumph. In their next game they beat Finland to clinch the gold medal. The underdogs were top dogs.

16

1982
CLARK MAKES "THE CATCH"

San Francisco 49ers wide receiver Dwight Clark was 6 feet 4 inches tall and had springs for legs. On January 10, 1982, he used every inch of his height and leaping ability to make a catch for the ages.

San Francisco was facing the Dallas Cowboys in the National Football Conference (NFC) Championship Game. The 49ers had looked sloppy. They had turned the ball over six times. They trailed 27–21 with 4:54 remaining when they got the ball back at their own 11-yard line.

Then quarterback Joe Montana became Joe Cool. In 12 plays he moved his team to the Dallas 6. There

Dwight Clark stretches to make "The Catch" against the Dallas Cowboys in the NFC Championship Game.

Malcolm Butler, *center*, saves the Super Bowl for the
New England Patriots.

the 49ers faced third-and-three with 58 seconds left.
Montana took the snap and rolled to his right, looking
for receiver Freddie Solomon. When he could not find
Solomon, Montana thought about throwing the ball
away. Then he saw Clark in the back of the end zone.
Under heavy pressure, Montana lofted the ball on

a high arc. Clark went up, stretched, caught it, and came down with both feet in bounds for a touchdown.

"If he doesn't catch it, nobody does," said Montana of his high pass. "But I have great confidence in Dwight's leaping ability."

The play became known simply as "The Catch." It gave the 49ers a 28–27 victory and their first NFC title. Two weeks later they beat the Cincinnati Bengals 26–21 in the Super Bowl.

BUTLER BAILS OUT PATRIOTS

On February 1, 2015, the Seattle Seahawks were a yard away from winning their second straight Super Bowl. But the New England Patriots had other ideas. Seattle trailed 28–24 with 20 seconds left. Quarterback Russell Wilson threw a quick pass, but cornerback Malcolm Butler jumped in front of the receiver to make a game-saving interception.

6

1982
CAL WINS ON "THE PLAY"

Stanford appeared to have scored a huge college football victory over archrival California in 1982. A field goal with four seconds to go had given Stanford a 20–19 lead. It would take something crazy for Cal to win.

"Crazy" does not do it justice. In one of the most bizarre endings in the history of college football, Cal returned Stanford's kickoff for a touchdown and a 25–20 victory. It was how the Golden Bears did it that was special. Cal lateraled the ball five times before scoring. It's known simply as "The Play."

Stanford guarded against a long return by kicking the ball short to the slower Cal blockers. The Bears'

California players Kevin Moen and Keith Kartz celebrate their stunning victory over Stanford in 1982.

Stanford band members charge the field early, thinking their team had beaten California in 1982.

Kevin Moen picked up the ball at his own 43-yard line. He threw a backward pass to Richard Rodgers, a faster teammate. Rodgers moved ahead but passed the ball back to Cal's Dwight Garner when he ran out of room. Garner gained a few yards, then pitched the ball back to Rodgers.

After crossing midfield, Rodgers pitched the ball to teammate Mariet Ford, a quick wide receiver. Ford raced to the Stanford 28. As Cardinal tacklers approached, Ford blindly pitched the ball backward. It landed perfectly in Moen's hands.

Moen sprinted toward the end zone. He eluded tacklers and some members of the Stanford band who had come onto the field to celebrate too early. Moen crossed the goal line for the touchdown and knocked over a Stanford trombone player for good measure.

"They had their party too soon," said Cal coach Joe Kapp. "The game is 60 minutes, not 59 minutes and 56 seconds."

7

1992
LAETTNER
SAVES DUKE

Many have called it one of the best games ever in college basketball. On March 28, 1992, Duke defeated Kentucky 104–103 in overtime. The victory came in the East Regional final of the National Collegiate Athletic Association (NCAA) Tournament. It put Duke into the Final Four. But first, top-seeded Duke had to get past Kentucky, the number two seed in the East.

The game was memorable for many reasons. Kentucky rallied from 12 points down to force overtime. Plus the teams combined to make more than 60 percent of their shots. But what most remember about the game is Christian Laettner and "The Shot."

Christian Laettner, *left*, launches his game-winning shot over Kentucky's Deron Feldhaus.

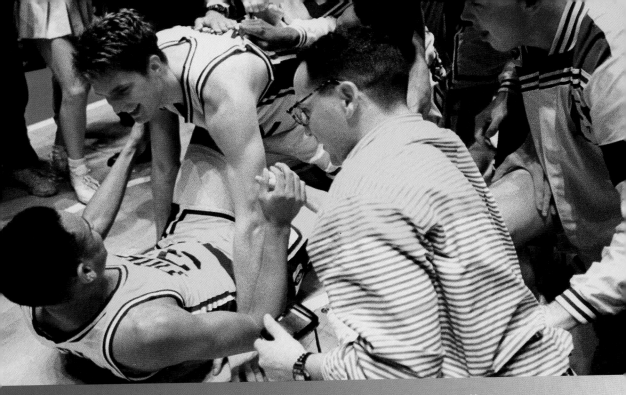

Grant Hill, *bottom*, and Christian Laettner are among the mob celebrating Duke's win over Kentucky in the 1992 NCAA East Regional final.

Laettner was Duke's senior All-American forward. He finished the day 10-for-10 from the field and 10-for-10 from the free-throw line. But Kentucky held a 103–102 lead with 2.1 seconds left in overtime. The Blue Devils had time for one last play. But they had to go the length of the court.

Duke's Grant Hill stood under his own basket. He took a couple steps to his right and heaved a one-handed pass down the court. The 6-foot-11 Laettner caught it near the free-throw line. He had just enough time to lean into his defender, dribble once and take a step back. He launched a high-arcing shot. The ball dropped through the net with no time left.

Joyful Duke players stormed the court. Kentucky's players were stunned. The Blue Devils had appeared to be finished. Instead they used their second chance and won their second straight national title.

WILD WOLFPACK

Two seconds remained in the 1983 NCAA basketball final between Houston and North Carolina State. The game was tied. State's Dereck Whittenburg heaved a desperate shot. It fell short, but right into the hands of teammate Lorenzo Charles. His dunk beat the buzzer, giving the Wolfpack a 54–52 upset of heavily favored Houston.

8

1996
STRUG'S GOLDEN VAULT

Kerri Strug was not the star of the 1996 US women's gymnastics team. Shannon Miller, Dominique Dawes, and Dominique Moceanu were the big names at the start of the Summer Olympics in Atlanta. That changed in a hurry. On July 23, 1996, Strug became the most famous gymnast in America.

The US women had never won the team gold medal. But going into their final apparatus of the competition, the Americans led Russia. A good score in the vault would earn them gold.

Yet after some disappointing routines, the gold medal was in doubt. Then it was Strug's turn. On her

US gymnastics coach Béla Károlyi carries Kerri Strug during the awards ceremony at the 1996 Olympic Games.

Kerri Strug grimaces after completing the vault that clinched the gold medal for Team USA.

first vault, she landed awkwardly and injured her left ankle. Her score was not high enough to guarantee gold, so US coach Béla Károlyi asked her to go again.

The 4-foot-9 Strug limped to the runway. The pain in her foot was intense. She vowed to do her best. She said a silent prayer: "Please, God, help me make this vault."

Strug put the pain out of her mind, sprinted down the runway, leaped, and did a back handspring. She landed on both feet as required, raised her left foot slightly, and held her pose. Then she collapsed in pain. But her score of 9.712 locked up the gold medal for Team USA.

"I have never seen such a moment," Károlyi said. "People think these girls are fragile dolls. They're not. They're courageous."

BEAMON GOES LONG

At the 1968 Summer Olympics in Mexico City, American Bob Beamon shocked the sports world. He shattered the world record in the long jump by almost two feet. He leaped 29 feet, 2 1/2 inches (8.90 m). The old record was 27 feet, 4 3/4 inches (8.35 m). Beamon's leap is still an Olympic record. It stood as the world record for 23 years.

1999 CHASTAIN BOOTS CHINA

On the afternoon of July 10, 1999, more than 90,000 fans filled the Rose Bowl. Most hoped to see the US women's soccer team beat China for the Women's World Cup championship.

Yet the game was still scoreless after 90 minutes of action. Neither team scored in two 15-minute overtimes. That sent the game to penalty kicks. Five players from each team would get a chance to score from 12 yards out against the opposing goalie. Chinese and US players took turns. The Americans would get the final shot.

US goalkeeper Briana Scurry stopped one of China's five shots. The first four Americans made theirs. Tied 4–4, US defender Brandi Chastain had the

Brandi Chastain's shot eludes China goalkeeper Gao Hong.

Women's World Cup title on her foot. A goal would mean a US championship. A miss would force sudden-death penalty shots.

"I felt the pressure," Chastain said. "But at the same time I was very confident."

Chastain kicked the ball with her left foot toward the right-hand corner of the net. The Chinese goalkeeper could not get a hand on it. Overjoyed, Chastain screamed, fell to her knees and pulled off her jersey. Her teammates swarmed her.

"It was just ecstasy," said Chastain. "It was satisfaction. It was relief. It was exhaustion. It was awesome."

2008
PHELPS BY A FINGERTIP

American swimmer Michael Phelps went to the 2008 Summer Olympics in Beijing, China, with the goal of winning eight gold medals. That would break the record of seven won by US swimmer Mark Spitz in 1972.

Phelps was only 23. Four years earlier in Athens, Greece, he had won six gold and two bronze medals.

Phelps was perfect in his first six races in Beijing. He set world records while winning four individual events. He was also part of two winning relays. But in his seventh race his dream almost came apart.

From the start of the 100-meter butterfly Phelps was in trouble. At the 50-meter turn he was in seventh place. He then began to overtake the others, one by

Michael Phelps charges hard in the 100-meter butterfly final at the 2008 Summer Olympics.

one. With 5 meters left, he was only inches behind Milorad Čavić of Serbia. That's when Phelps took one last, lunging stroke.

He and Čavić appeared to touch the wall at the same time. But the electronic timing device gave the victory to Phelps. When Phelps saw on the scoreboard he had won, he screamed and pounded his fists into the water. His amazing comeback had saved his medal quest. A review of the video upheld his victory by one one-hundredth of a second.

"It seems like every day I'm in a dream world," said Phelps, who would win his eighth gold in his next race. "Sometimes you have to pinch yourself to see if it's real."

2011
FREESE SAVES ST. LOUIS

Game 6 of the 2011 World Series had a little bit of everything and a double scoop of drama. The game between the St. Louis Cardinals and the Texas Rangers took 4 hours and 33 minutes to play. There were 19 runs, six home runs, and 15 pitchers used.

The Rangers needed just one win to clinch their first World Series title. Twice they came within one strike of closing out the Cardinals. But it proved to be a tough task.

St. Louis trailed 7–5 with two men on and two out in the bottom of the ninth. Cardinals third baseman David Freese faced Rangers closer Neftali Feliz.

David Freese pumps his arm as he rounds the bases after his home run won Game 6 of the 2011 World Series.

David Freese reacts after his ninth-inning triple tied Game 6 of the 2011 World Series.

With two strikes, Freese hit a two-run triple to tie the game and send it to extra innings.

In the top of the 10th inning, the Rangers scored two runs. In the bottom of the inning, the Cardinals again were down to their last strike when Lance Berkman singled to tie it again. In the bottom of the 11th inning, Freese gave St. Louis a 10–9 win with a leadoff home run over the center-field fence.

Earlier Freese had dropped a popup that cost the Cardinals a run. He finished as the hero. Freese drove in two more runs in the Game 7 victory and was named World Series Most Valuable Player (MVP) as St. Louis took home the title.

HOBBLING HERO

Injuries to both legs kept Kirk Gibson on the bench for Game 1 of the 1988 World Series. His Los Angeles Dodgers were down to their last out, trailing the Oakland Athletics 4–3. He was called on to pinch-hit against ace closer Dennis Eckersley. It looked like a mismatch. But with the count full and a runner on, Gibson hit a walk-off homer. The Dodgers won 5–4.

12

2013
THE MIAMI MIRACLE

In the history of the National Basketball Association (NBA), nobody has ever made more three-point shots than Ray Allen. Over 18 years, Allen made 2,973 three-pointers in the regular season. In 11 postseasons he made 385 more. Teammates and opponents marveled at his shooting skill.

"He's just a machine," said longtime coach Doc Rivers. Former teammate Antonio Daniels called him "probably the best pure shooter of all time."

Of all the three-pointers Allen made, none was bigger than one he made on June 18, 2013. It saved a season and led to a championship.

Ray Allen fires his game-tying shot over San Antonio's Tony Parker in Game 6 of the 2013 NBA Finals.

Allen's Miami Heat trailed the San Antonio Spurs three games to two in the NBA Finals. With 19.4 seconds remaining in Game 6, the Spurs led 95–92. A victory would give San Antonio the title.

Miami's LeBron James missed a three-pointer. The Heat's Chris Bosh grabbed the rebound and passed the ball to Allen in the corner. Allen took a step behind the three-point line. He lofted a high shot over a charging defender. The ball swished through the net with 5.2 seconds remaining to tie the game.

The Heat won in overtime. Then they won Game 7 to claim the NBA title.

"It's going to be a shot that I'm going to remember for a long time," Allen said.

The Miami crowd goes wild after Ray Allen sent Game 6 of the 2013 NBA Finals into overtime.

13

2013
TIGERS SHOCK THE TIDE

The first time Auburn and Alabama played a football game was in 1893. In the years since, both schools had become football powers. They developed a fierce in-state rivalry. Each season the Auburn-Alabama game is called the Iron Bowl. Though many of those games have been exciting, none had a more memorable ending than the one on November 30, 2013.

Top-ranked and undefeated Alabama built a 21–7 lead in the second quarter. But Auburn fought back. The Tigers tied the game 28–28 with 32 seconds left in the fourth quarter. Alabama then drove to the Auburn 38 with one second remaining. The Crimson Tide set up for a 57-yard field goal. Head coach Nick Saban

Chris Davis sprints down the sideline to score the game-winning touchdown for Auburn against Alabama in 2013.

figured his team would either make the kick and win or go to overtime.

Instead, something unexpected happened. Kicker Adam Griffith's kick was just short. Auburn's Chris Davis caught it a yard from the back of his own end zone. Davis started running up the center of the field. He then cut left behind a wall of blockers. He raced down the sideline past midfield. He broke into the clear and could not be caught. Davis's 109-yard touchdown gave Auburn a 34–28 victory.

HONORABLE MENTIONS

Bobby Thomson—Hit a three-run home run in the bottom of the ninth to give the New York Giants a 5–4 victory over the Brooklyn Dodgers in the final game of a best-of-three playoff to decide the 1951 National League pennant.

Willie Mays—Robbed Cleveland's Vic Wertz with a remarkable catch in Game 1 of the 1954 World Series. The Giants center fielder's over-the-shoulder catch with two on and nobody out in the eighth inning of a 2–2 game sparked a four-game sweep of the Indians.

Franco Harris—Caught a deflected pass and ran for a touchdown to complete a 60-yard play in the final seconds as the Pittsburgh Steelers defeated the Oakland Raiders 13–7 in a 1972 AFC playoff game.

Jack Nicklaus—At age 46, the Golden Bear posted a score of 30 (6-under par) over the final nine holes of the final round of the 1986 Masters to clinch his eighteenth and final major championship.

Keith Smart—Sank a 16-foot shot from the corner with four seconds left in the 1987 NCAA basketball championship game, giving Indiana a 74–73 victory over Syracuse.

Pat LaFontaine—Scored in the fourth overtime of a 1987 Game 7 playoff game—6 hours and 18 minutes after it began—lifting the New York Islanders past the Washington Capitals 3–2.

Michael Jordan—Hit a 20-foot jump shot with 5.2 seconds left in Game 6 of the 1998 NBA Finals. The basket gave the Chicago Bulls an 87–86 victory over the Utah Jazz and clinched Chicago's sixth title in eight years.

GLOSSARY

closer
A baseball team's best relief pitcher, generally used to protect small leads in the ninth inning.

Final Four
The last four teams remaining at the end of the NCAA basketball tournament.

lateral
A parallel or backward pass in a football game.

perfect game
A baseball game in which a pitcher retires all 27 batters he faces.

pinch hitter
In baseball, a player who is sent into the game to bat for a player already in the lineup.

rivalry
A matchup between teams that especially want to beat one another because of their history.

walk-off
A play that wins a baseball game in the bottom half of the last inning, allowing the teams to walk off the field.

FOR MORE INFORMATION

Books

Myers, Gary. *The Catch: One Play, Two Dynasties, and the Game That Changed the NFL*. New York: Three Rivers Press, 2010.

Peters, Stephanie True. *Great Moments in the Summer Olympics*. New York: Little, Brown, 2012.

Rappoport, Ken, and Barry Wilner. *The Big Dance: The Story of the NCAA Basketball Tournament*. Lanham, MD: Taylor Trade Publishing, 2012.

Websites

To learn more about the Legendary World of Sports, visit **booklinks.abdopublishing.com**. These links are routinely monitored and updated to provide the most current information available.

INDEX

ABOUT THE AUTHOR

Doug Williams is a freelance writer in San Diego. He is a former newspaper reporter and editor. He has written several books about sports and writes for many national and San Diego-area publications. He enjoys reading, hiking, and spending time with his family.